YOUR KNOWLEDGE HAS VALUE

- We will publish your bachelor's and master's thesis, essays and papers

- Your own eBook and book -
  sold worldwide in all relevant shops

- Earn money with each sale

Upload your text at www.GRIN.com
and publish for free

Bibliographic information published by the German National Library:

The German National Library lists this publication in the National Bibliography; detailed bibliographic data are available on the Internet at http://dnb.dnb.de .

This book is copyright material and must not be copied, reproduced, transferred, distributed, leased, licensed or publicly performed or used in any way except as specifically permitted in writing by the publishers, as allowed under the terms and conditions under which it was purchased or as strictly permitted by applicable copyright law. Any unauthorized distribution or use of this text may be a direct infringement of the author s and publisher s rights and those responsible may be liable in law accordingly.

Imprint:

Copyright © 2018 GRIN Verlag
Print and binding: Books on Demand GmbH, Norderstedt Germany
ISBN: 9783668703971

This book at GRIN:

https://www.grin.com/document/425087

Brandon Holladay

Hurricane Katrina and the Flooding of New Orleans. A Natural Disaster and its Consequences

GRIN Verlag

GRIN - Your knowledge has value

Since its foundation in 1998, GRIN has specialized in publishing academic texts by students, college teachers and other academics as e-book and printed book. The website www.grin.com is an ideal platform for presenting term papers, final papers, scientific essays, dissertations and specialist books.

Visit us on the internet:

http://www.grin.com/

http://www.facebook.com/grincom

http://www.twitter.com/grin_com

Hurricane Katrina And the Flooding of New Orleans (2005)

Briefly

Hurricane Katrina is tied with Hurricane Harvey as being the costliest tropical cyclones in history. The storm was immense with a range of over 400 miles wide and winds of 140 miles per hour or more making landfall as a Category 3 hurricane. Though the storm was immense, the aftermath would be the demonstration of a catastrophe. The failures that contributed to a city being underwater for weeks to follow is one of the greatest disasters associated with this hurricane.

The cost of the storm and its aftermath would be felt for years to come. The total mount of property damage is estimated at 125 billion dollars (2005 USD). This is roughly four times the amount of damage caused by the Hurricane Andrew which happened in 1992. 1245-1836 people killed is the estimated total as this counts evacuees on the latter end of the amount as people who were classified as missing which makes an exact number hard to determine (Heerden, 2007, p. 24).

Introduction

New Orleans is a city for which nearly all of its footprint lies below sea level and relies upon an extensive levee and flood wall system to protect the city from flooding. This system would be a catalyst for which caused New Orleans to severely damaged by Hurricane Katrina's storm surge (Cigler, 2007, p. 65). The United States Army Corp of Engineers was the responsible party for design and construction of the levee system while the local levee boards are charged with the maintenance of the levee system.

As Hurricane Katrina is getting closer to making landfall, the levee system designed to protect New Orleans was only 60-90% complete, the design was also inadequate and was about to be exposed. As the canals rose with storm surge, the levee system failed in six major locations but over 50 locations around the New Orleans area. In some locations where the breeches occurred were significantly below designed levels.

Flooding became a significant worry following a few significant events in New Orleans. Hurricane Betsy in 1965 helped to spread awareness of the impact of flooding and helped established the Flood Control Act of 1965. The act placed the burden of design and construction on the U.S. Army Corp of Engineers (USACE) and local levee governing bodies will be responsible for maintenance. The Flood Control Act of 1965 included New Orleans in the areas needing this infrastructure of flood protection (Heerden, 2007, p. 26).

Also that same year, Congress authorized the Lake Pontchartrain and Vicinity Hurricane Protection Project (LPVHPP) which restated the principle of local participation in federally funded projects. The project was estimated to take around thirteen years, but when Hurricane Katrina wreaked havoc in 2005, almost four decades later, the project was only 60–90% complete with a revised projected completion date of 2015 (Cigler, 2007, p. 67).

The Setting

Since the founding of New Orleans in the 18th century, there has always been the need to be concerned with drainage as the city is in unique circumstances. The unique geographically environment is rare as the entire city is mostly surrounded by water: Lake Pontchartrain to the North, Lake Borgne to the East, wetlands to the East and West respectively, and the Mississippi River is located to the South of city (Cigler, 2007, p. 65). This coupled with the city being at or below sea level in most places and no natural exit point for water maintains the water is expelled by evaporation or pumping.

Pumping has been the most significant method to relieve water from the city since earlier times in history. Shortcomings such as the need for electricity was one of the first failures of the pumping system, diesel pumps were introduced following the Great Flood of 1927 (Heerden, 2007, p. 25). Hurricane Katrina would prove to the greatest failure for the pumping system, leaving most of the pumps submerged or without power or fuel to run them. Typically in disasters what can go wrong will go wrong at the worst possible time.

Disaster Unfolds

On August 29, 2005, the worst disaster ever to impact the flood control infrastructure in New Orleans was preparing to make landfall as a Category 3 Hurricane. It's important to note that Katrina did not flood the city rather the storm surge identified design flaws in the levee system. One of the breaches which was catastrophic was the 17th Street Canal failure as this was used to pump flood water out of the city and when it breached, it also submerged the drainage system causing the entire system to fail (Nicholson & Silva-Tulla, 2008, p. 127).

Water began to come up through the flood drains in parts of the city which were still dry and had pumped water out. The following day 80% of the city was under water and with the pumping stations submerged or without fuel or electricity to run as well being inaccessible due to the widespread flooding turning them back on would be impossible (Heerden, 2007, p. 24).

The levee failures would prove to be the cause of the greatest engineering disaster in U.S. history as it was billed as. Many of the breaches were below designed specifications such as with the 17th Street Canal which was four feet below designs specifications when it failed (Nicholson & Silva-Tulla, 2008, p. 127). Some were overtopped which like earthen dams once over topping occurs scouring and erosion usually quickly follow and cause complete failure shortly after (Ebersole, Dean, & Hughes, 2011, p. 359).

By August 31, as the flooding equalized to Lake Pontchartrain, water began to flow out however though inadequacies in the levee systems which caused the breaches, they actually retained much of the water in the city. The breaches had to be fixed before the water could be pumped out due to the pumping stations being submerged or inaccessible due to the flooding (O'Neill, 2008, p. 101). Weeks would pass before the water was able to be pumped out of the city.

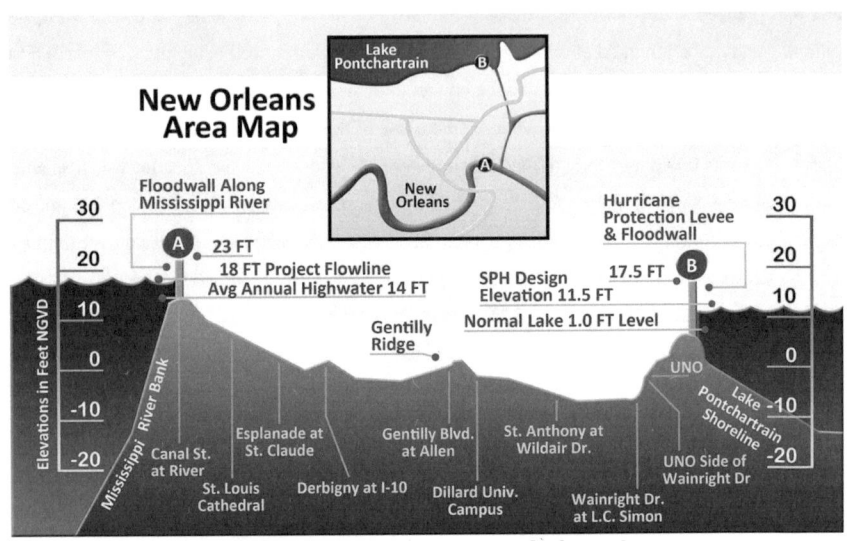

City of New Orleans Ground Elevations
From Canal St. at the Mississippi River to the Lakefront at U.N.O.

https://upload.wikimedia.org/wikipedia/commons/thumb/b/b2/New_Orleans_Elevations.jpg/1280px-New_Orleans_Elevations.jpg

Impact

After the failure of the levees and flood walls, the pumping system and drainage was rendered basically useless as many stations were submerged or ran out of fuel without the accessibility to refuel them and the canals having been breached were back-flowing back into the city (O'Neill, 2008, p. 101). The flood control was a total loss in an emergency management standpoint as any logistics to bring response and relief in had to come by boat or air.

Eighty percent of the city was underwater for weeks to come until the levee breaches could be repaired and the pumping stations could be restarted. Some of the water would have flowed back into Lake Pontchartrain had the levees not been there but they retained water inside of the city. This would be further complicated by more flooding after Hurricane Rita which hit a few weeks later (Cigler, 2007, p.71). Most of the water would be out of the city by late October.

Though the water had receded, the destruction was just beginning to be seen. Most houses and businesses having been under such a depth of water and for such an extensive amount of time, they were deemed total losses most of the time. Some of the pumps could not be restarted as the wiring had been underwater for so long causing corrosion. Some pumps would fail at a later time also due to be in brackish water for so long.

Containing the Disaster

The disaster of flooding on New Orleans was relatively contained in a sense as the flood walls which failed held much of that same water in and released very slowly. The disaster in New Orleans was not able to contained to any part of the city below sea level as the loss of flood control through walls and levees caused the pumping stations to fail as well as the stations would have only been able to loop the water as the canals they pumped into were breached (Wang & Castay, 2008, p. 812).

Lacking a natural exit due to gravity of being below sea level, pumping and evaporation were the only ways for the water to be removed from the city. Flood drains became the path of least resistance moving the water to areas of the city which had initially been free from the immense flooding.

Relief and First Response Efforts

The response effort was one of the most criticized areas involving the devastation to New Orleans. The governor Ray Nagin was not prepared for the magnitude of Katrina, waiting until the day before landfall to establish a mandatory emergency evacuation. There is also the inability to secure food and basic needs for those who sought refuge in these last resort shelters.

The SuperDome, home to the New Orleans Saints, was setup as a shelter since it was above flooding level. It did withstand significant roof damage during the time when high winds had hit New Orleans. There is a photograph earlier in the article which shows the mass amounts of people who took refuge in the stadium, and also the areas of triage which were established inside by first responders and relief personnel.

Aftermath and Investigation into the Disaster

The aftermath and investigations into the disaster sought to find the contributing factors which led to the failure of the flood control systems. The 17th Street Canal was one of the problem areas as an investigated into the design of the levee system there and that it was destined to fail due to the design utilized by the USACE as mentioned earlier, it was one of the levees which had failed below capacity (Wang & Castay, 2008, p. 812). The soil strength was miscalculated and was one of the key issues which contributed to the failure of this canal (Nicholson & Silva-Tulla, 2008, p. 126).

The USACE would later install flood gates which would prevent Lake Pontchartrain from back-flowing into the city in a similar circumstance, however this also severely limits how much water can be pumped out of the city during a flood. It seems nearly any technology utilized will be negative to one aspect of the flood control system and a benefit to another aspect to the flood control system in and around New Orleans (Wang & Castay, 2012, p. 813).

Several of the levees failed due to being overtopped. Since they were made of materials which would erode very quickly if overtopped. There were also notions that the levees has been improperly maintained by the local levee boards. There was the discovery of sand used instead of the thicker Louisiana Clay (Ebersole, Dean, & Hughes, 2011, p. 359). The lack of completed infrastructure as much the flood control infrastructure started three decades earlier had not been finished and had been rescheduled to be finished by 2015.

Lessons Learned and Policy Impact

One of the lessons learned was the importance of flood control and the soundness of that flood control infrastructure. The design and construction had began more than three decades before and had not been finished by the time in which Hurricane Katrina happened. The flaws in the design of the levee system had not been exposed before due to the pumping stations doing their jobs and not testing the capacity of the levee system.

Another lesson learned was the redundancy of the pumping stations which couldn't run without diesel fuel or that they became marooned without a route to refuel them. There also wasn't the addressing of the possibility that the pumps may become submerged in water. The pumping stations were the only way to get water out of New Orleans other than through merely evaporation.

Throughout the history of the city pump stations have continued to become overwhelmed signifying an area which upon failure will the leave the city without a way to drain excess water.

The local levees board and the USACE have severe communication issues. The construction and progress was not maintained over the three decades since construction started on probably the largest threat to city of New Orleans which is flooding. Storm drains also worked against the city as they acted as piping to other areas of the city which had remained dry and had pumped their water out.

Implications for Modern Emergency Management

It's important to understand the modern implications of a disaster such as this. The failure of Flood Control Infrastructure of New Orleans during Hurricane Katrina exhibits certain scenarios or policy implications which need to be reviewed and understood as to prevent future events which share the commonality of issues in similar disasters.

The importance of maintaining the pumping stations in a city prone to flooding or below sea level without natural exit points is important to begin response and recovery and reestablishing utilities and logistical route for aid. Having back up fuel reserves or power sources to be able to utilize pumps to dispel water is important to the goal of bringing down floodwaters. There also must be adequate protection to prevent the submerging of these pumps. There is also the need to maintain a logistical way to deliver fuel to these stations as to prevent them from becoming unusable in extended situations without access to electricity.

Flood wall and levee systems need to be stress tested and inspected routinely to identify certain problems areas which could contribute to their failure. Scenarios such as breeched levees have to be utilized to understand how one failure can impact the rest of the system or how it can be detrimental to drainage systems. Also the completion of upgrades or construction has to be in a timely manner as mentioned earlier some of the projects were not finished over three decades. Disasters can occur at any time, so there is a necessity to be prepared in the most apt manner to prevent damage or loss.

Summary

Even though the catastrophic failures of the system which was designed to protect the city of New Orleans, the importance of flood control is reiterated. The design of levees and flood control walls have to be designed to be able to withstand capacity and in the event of failure of them all secondary effects have to be considered. The entire drainage system was either unusable due to pumping stations being submerged or unable to be powered and the storm drains acted as a conduit to send water to dry areas as a path of least resistance.

It's also important to how a complex plan in place in the event of a disaster of such a magnitude such as ways to get fuel in for pumping stations, having resources to repair levee breaches, and having the resources needed to maintain a population with basic human needs in an environment which may take an extended time to bring back to pre disaster condition.

References

Cigler, B. A. (2007). The "big questions" of katrina and the 2005 great flood of new orleans. Public Administration Review, 67(S1), 64-76.

Ebersole, B. A., Dean, R. G., & Hughes, S. A. (2011). Discussion of "Simulated wave-induced erosion of the mississippi River–Gulf outlet levees during hurricane katrina" by rune storesund, robert G. bea, and yuli huang. Journal of Waterway, Port, Coastal, and Ocean Engineering, 136;137;(6), 355-360. doi:10.1061/(ASCE)WW.1943-5460.0000083

Ivor Ll. van Heerden. (2007). The failure of the new orleans levee system following hurricane katrina and the pathway forward. Public Administration Review, 67(S1), 24-35. doi:10.1111/j.1540-6210.2007.00810.x

Nicholson, P., & Silva-Tulla, F. (2008). Reconnaissance of levee failures after hurricane katrina. Proceedings of the Institution of Civil Engineers - Civil Engineering, 161(3), 124-131. doi:10.1680/cien.2008.161.3.124

O'Neill, K. M. (2008). Broken levees, broken lives, and a broken nation after hurricane katrina. Southern Cultures, 14(2), 89-108. doi:10.1353/scu.0.0001

Wang, X., & Castay, M. (2012). Failure analysis of the breached levee at the 17th street canal in new orleans during hurricane katrina. Canadian Geotechnical Journal, 49(7), 812-834. doi:10.1139/t2012-043

Ubilla, J., Abdoun, T., Sasanakul, I., Sharp, M., Steedman, S., Vanadit-Ellis, W., & Zimmie, T. (2008). New orleans levee system performance during hurricane katrina: London avenue and orleans canal south. Journal of Geotechnical and Geoenvironmental Engineering, 134(5), 668-680. doi:10.1061/(ASCE)1090-0241(2008)134:5(668)

YOUR KNOWLEDGE HAS VALUE

- We will publish your bachelor's and master's thesis, essays and papers

- Your own eBook and book - sold worldwide in all relevant shops

- Earn money with each sale

Upload your text at www.GRIN.com
and publish for free